To

Dad,
Happy Fathers Day! Love Always,
Kim + Erin

MW00744508

For our fathers

A FATHER IS SOMEONE WHO . . .

by Nick Beilenson
and Laurence L. Beilenson

Illustrated by Andrew Toos

PETER PAUPER PRESS, INC.
WHITE PLAINS, NEW YORK

A FATHER IS SOMEONE WHO . . .

- never remembers the camera, but takes credit for all the good photos.

- thinks changing a diaper and giving his child a bath on the same day means automatic induction into the Fathers' Hall of Fame.

- goes to bed earlier than his teen-aged kids.

A Father Is Someone Who . . . looks on the lighter side of what can be serious business. Today's up-to-date, cool, sensitive, and politically correct father sometimes teeters on the balance beam of life, and often has to rush in where angels fear to tread. What with coaching soccer, washing the dishes, and making a living, the modern father plays many roles in a life that is partly high drama and partly low farce.

So fathers, turn the page and . . . THIS IS YOUR LIFE!

N.B. and L.L.B.

A FATHER IS SOMEONE WHO . . .

―――――――――――― ❧⸙ ――――――――――――

is the king of his castle . . .
sand, that is.

A FATHER IS SOMEONE WHO ...

makes the word "weekend"
a source of excitement for his children.

A Father is Someone Who ...

thinks his two-year-old who says
six words is a genius.

A Father is Someone Who . . .

thinks five minutes alone when he comes home
from work is better than a vacation.

A FATHER IS SOMEONE WHO . . .

thinks changing a diaper and giving his child a bath
on the same day means automatic induction
into the Fathers' Hall of Fame.

A FATHER IS SOMEONE WHO . . .

says "it's how you play the game,"
but loves it when you win.

A Father is Someone Who ...

⚜

can teach you how to fill out a baseball scorecard,
but can't find the car in the parking lot.

A FATHER IS SOMEONE WHO . . .

forgives and forgets
(he has Mom to remember).

A Father is Someone Who ...

lets you know he thinks graduation
from kindergarten is an important event.

A FATHER IS SOMEONE WHO ...

thinks that youth soccer is more fun than
pro sports—if his daughter is in the game.

A Father is Someone Who . . .

believes the coach who tells him
his seven-year-old is headed for
the Big Leagues.

A FATHER IS SOMEONE WHO ...

thinks he's a radical dude
if his tie has more than two colors.

A FATHER IS SOMEONE WHO ...

———————— ❧❧ ————————

never makes you walk the dog
on a stormy night.

A FATHER IS SOMEONE WHO ...

may get old before his time—
and has his children to thank.

A FATHER IS SOMEONE WHO ...

gets annoyed when you do what he does,
not what he says.

A FATHER IS SOMEONE WHO ...

---

thinks you are the best gift
he ever received.

A FATHER IS SOMEONE WHO . . .

=================== ❧❧ ===================

has "one handicap"—and it applies
to his golf game.

A FATHER IS SOMEONE WHO . . .

can always solve homework problems . . .
until the sixth grade.

A Father is Someone Who . . .

lets you eat off his plate
when Mom isn't looking.

A FATHER IS SOMEONE WHO ...

always lets the kids win, and then one day
realizes he has no choice.

A Father is Someone Who ...

thinks he should get an Oscar for successfully
taping a late-night movie on the VCR.

A FATHER IS SOMEONE WHO ...

stands like a rock on matters of principle—
such as whether to go to McDonald's.

A FATHER IS SOMEONE WHO ...

needs his child's help
to turn on the computer.

A FATHER IS SOMEONE WHO . . .

is a bank where you
don't need an ATM card.

A FATHER IS SOMEONE WHO . . .

lets his daughter order the most expensive
thing on the menu, just as he did.

A FATHER IS SOMEONE WHO . . .

——— ❧❧ ———

coaches lacrosse in the morning, baseball at noon,
and soccer in the afternoon—and has
only two children.

A FATHER IS SOMEONE WHO . . .

goes to bed earlier
than his teen-aged kids.

A Father is Someone Who ...

❧⸱❧

catches himself reading *Peter Rabbit*
to his wife at bedtime.

A Father is Someone Who ...

knows the best route to
the hospital emergency room.

A FATHER IS SOMEONE WHO ...

is careful with his kids' diet, making sure they
get the FDA-required daily allowance
of hot dogs and ice cream.

A FATHER IS SOMEONE WHO ...

can't understand what the teacher
could possibly want to talk to him about.

A FATHER IS SOMEONE WHO . . .

if he doesn't have something nice to say,
offers constructive criticism.

A FATHER IS SOMEONE WHO . . .

thinks red is a performance option
when buying the family station wagon.

A FATHER IS SOMEONE WHO . . .

when the going gets tough, says,
"Ask your mother."

A FATHER IS SOMEONE WHO ...

━━━━━━━━━━━ ❧❧ ━━━━━━━━━━━

is capable of making hamburgers any way
they're ordered—as long as it's well done.

A Father is Someone Who ...

likes to relive past sporting triumphs—
like the time he caught a foul ball barehanded
(after it beaned the poor guy two rows in front of him).

A FATHER IS SOMEONE WHO . . .

loves his children
so much it hurts.